6. Pray for God's help. You *need* God's help in order to understand what you study in the Bible. PSALM 119:18 would be an appropriate verse for you to take to God in prayer.

7. *Class teachers using this course for group study will find some helpful suggestions on*

how to
take the self-check

Each lesson is concluded with a test designed to help you evaluate what you have learned.

1. Review the lesson carefully in the light of the self-check test questions.

2. If there are any questions in the self-check test you cannot answer, perhaps you have written into your lesson the wrong answer from your Bible. Go over your work carefully to make sure you have filled in the blanks correctly.

3. When you think you are ready to take the self-check test, do so without looking up the answers.

4. Check your answers to the self-check test carefully with the answer key given on page 80.

5. If you have any questions wrong, your answer key will tell you where to find the correct answers in your lesson. Go back and locate the right answers. Learn by your mistakes!

apply
what you have learned
to your own life

In this connection, read carefully JAMES 1:22-25. It is only as you apply your lessons to your own life that you will really grow in grace and increase in the knowledge of God.

Introduction to Romans

Place of writing

Probably Corinth, or nearby Cenchrea.

1. Who was Paul's host while he was in Corinth?
ROMANS 16:23; compare I CORINTHIANS 1:14_____

2. Who was probably the mail carrier who took Paul's letter to the Christians at Rome?
ROMANS 16:1, 2_____

Date of writing

About spring of A.D. 58. Paul had been a Christian about twenty years.

Occasion of writing

3. What great desire of Paul's heart had long been unsatisfied?
ROMANS 1:9-13; compare 15:22-29_____

_____

(The epistle was to pave the way for his coming and supply much-needed teaching material.)

Contents

A philosophy of the gospel, showing how it meets every human need and is the only answer to the problem of the guilt and power of sin.

4. What is the theme of the book?

ROMANS 1:16, 17_____

Simple outline

Chapters 1—8 Doctrinal

Chapters 9-11 Dispensational

Chapters 12-16 Practical

Detailed outline

(This course follows the outline below.)

Introduction or prologue (1:1-17)

Righteousness needed by sinful men (1:18—3:20)

    Heathen (1:18-32)

    Moralizer (2:1-16)

    Jew (2:17—3:8)

    World (3:9-20)

Righteousness provided by God (3:21-26)

Righteousness received by faith (3:27—4:25)

Righteousness experienced in the soul (5:1—8:17)

Righteousness guaranteed a permanent blessing (8:18-39)

Righteousness rejected by Jews (chapters 9—11)

Righteousness manifested in daily life (chapters 12—16)

Prologue (Romans 1:1-17)

One can hardly escape the fact that this letter is something infinitely more than a human production. It is an oracle of God, a revelation of eternal facts.

Read ROMANS 1:1-4 before answering the following questions.

5. Note expression in 1:1—"gospel of God." Three other keys using the title "God" are found in verses 16, 17, 18.

_____of God (verse 16),_____of

God (verse 17),_____of God (verse 18).

6. To what extent was the gospel of an all-sufficient sacrifice "promised afore" in the Old Testament?

ROMANS 1:2, 3; LUKE 24:26, 27_____

_____

7. What was seen by "all the prophets"?

ACTS 10:43_____

_____

The hope of Israel was brought to an intense pitch in the days just prior to the birth of Jesus, yet the Jews, because of their misconceptions of such passages as ISAIAH 53, rejected Him.

8. The beginning of ROMANS (1:3), the beginning of the New Testament (MATTHEW 1:1) and almost its end (REVELATION 22:16), and the close of Paul's ministry (II TIMOTHY 2:8), all emphasize that the Saviour is the son (or seed) of whom?

_____

9. While Jesus on the human side was the seed of David, what contrasting truth do we have in ROMANS 1:4?

_____

10. Jesus declared ("marked out by sure signs") to be the Son of God with_____as demonstrated by His

_____. 1:4

Read ROMANS 1:5-13.

11. Who were equally the givers of eternal blessing?

1:7_____

12. What is every Christian called to be?

1:7_____

4

13. Who are defined as "saints"?

PSALM 50:5_____

_____

14. What had Paul wanted to do for a long time?

ROMANS 1:13_____

We find on more than one occasion that Paul's most deliberate plans were subject to divine correction. It was not Paul who was inspired, but the record he gave us of divine truth.

Read ROMANS 1:14-17.

15. What were two familiar divisions of mankind in Paul's day?

1:14_____

Barbarus—speaker of an unintelligible tongue—any language not Greek. "Greek and Barbarian" comprehended the Gentile world.

16. What was Paul ready to do?

1:15_____

17. Did Paul recognize some limitations on his ability to do this?

1:15_____

The measure in which we are conscious of limitation is usually the measure in which we make possible the operation of the Holy Spirit through us.

18. Why was Paul not ashamed to preach this gospel anywhere?

1:16_____

_____

19. If the gospel is foolishness to some people, what is it to others?

I Corinthians 1:18, 24_____

_____

20. In what therefore does the faith of a believer stand?

I Corinthians 2:5_____

The Greek word *dunamis,* here translated "power," gives us our word *dynamite* (explosive power). The gospel is the dynamite of God (Psalm 62:11). Moral reform and social schemes are impotent to penetrate human wickedness. The gospel overcomes the greatest resistance, penetrates the hardest conscience, softens the most obstinate heart.

21. By what do we have access to God?

Romans 5:2_____

22. By what are we justified?

Romans 3:28_____

23. By what do we live?

Romans 1:17_____

24. Since man is incapable of attaining the righteousness of the law, the gospel offers him a righteous standing in Christ, received by faith, after which righteousness is produced in

life by _____

_____. Romans 8:3, 4

check-up time No. 1

*You have now finished the prologue of Romans.
Review the questions and your written answers.
You may use the following self-check test in your
review. If you are uncertain of an answer, reread
the Scripture text to see if you can find the answer. Then take this test to see how well you understand and remember the truths you have
studied thus far.*

*In the right-hand margin write "True" or "False"
after each of the following statements.*

1. There are four keys in the first eighteen
verses of Romans 1, like "gospel of God." _____

2. The gospel of a sufficient sacrifice for sin was
foreseen in the Old Testament. _____

3. The prophets spoke of the remission of sins
through the Messiah (Christ). _____

4. According to Romans 1, Christ was of the
seed of David. _____

5. The resurrection of Christ was associated
with power. _____

6. All true believers are saints. _____

7. Paul's personal plans were always inspired. _____

8. The two familiar divisions of mankind in
Paul's day were Greeks and Barbarians. _____

9. Salvation is by faith. _____

10. Paul says he was ashamed of the gospel. _____

Turn to page 80 and check your answers.

Righteousness Needed by Sinful Man

(Romans 1:18—3:20)

The heathen condemned (Romans 1:18-32)

Read ROMANS 1:18-20.

1. What is revealed as well as the righteousness of God?

1:18_____

2. Against what two traits is it revealed?

1:18_____

Note the last phrase of verse 18: "Who hold. . . ." This is literally "hold down" or suppress the truth, living in unrighteousness as a result. Many a man has personal reasons for not wanting to believe in future retribution.

3. On whom does the wrath of God abide?

JOHN 3:36_____

4. The unsaved are called children_____.

_____EPHESIANS 2:3

God never ceases to be love, but love sometimes has to hurt. As the adversary of evil, God must have wrath. But it is the wrath of a righteous Judge, not an arbitrary outburst of passion.

5. "Thy judgments_____." PSALM 119:75

6. But how can God hold the "uninstructed" heathen accountable?

ROMANS 1:19_____

_____

7. What things in particular has He revealed to all men?

1:20_____

8. What is concrete proof that there is an all-wise and all-powerful God?

1:20_____

Read ROMANS 1:21-23.

9. Even when men see evidences of God, what causes them to turn their backs upon Him?

1:21_____

_____

The word for *imaginations* means "thinkings"—free thought. Skepticism is simply the result of biased thinking and a "foolish" (literally "unintelligent") heart.

10. How does this foolishness of the professedly wise often manifest itself?

1:23_____

Read ROMANS 1:24-32.

11. When men give themselves over to_____

_____(EPHESIANS 4:19), God gives them up to

_____. ROMANS 1:24

Sin will be punished by its own proper results. It is a dire thought that God must give some men up to their own counsels. From the human viewpoint, it is the working out of a natural process. From the divine viewpoint, it is retribution from God. God has so constituted these natural processes that evil gravitates to wretchedness.

12. God is not mocked, for _____

_____. GALATIANS 6:7

We turn now from the awful exposure of heathen sin to an examination of the moralizer, either a heathen Gentile or a Jew, who condemns others and justifies himself.

The moralizer condemned (Romans 2:1-16)

Read ROMANS 2:1-6.

13. Although the moralizer might condemn the heathen for their gross sins, what problem did he face himself?

2:1_____

14. On what basis does God judge all men?

2:2_____

(The word for *truth* here means "reality." Being a relatively moral man does not mean that he is free from sin.)

15. What is one of the worst sins in the sight of God?

2:4_____

_____

16. We have redemption according to _____

_____. EPHESIANS 1:7, 8

Read ROMANS 2:7-11.

17. Is the doctrine of salvation by faith something that encourages loose conduct?

2:7_____

18. What is the certain fate of those who are unregenerate, whether Jew or Gentile?

"Indignation and _____" (2:8). "Tribulation and

_____." 2:9

19. Who has a special priority on this tribulation and wrath?

2:9 _____ And on the fruits of salvation?

2:10_____

20. What vital fact should lay hold of us all?

2:11_____

Read ROMANS 2:12-16.

21. Can listening to the law or approving of it save any one?

2:12_____

22. Does a heathen who has never heard the law have a certain amount of light to which God can hold him accountable?

2:14_____

While there is one principle of judgment for all, judgment must be based upon light. The standard to which the Jew could be held was the Mosaic law. The Gentile still had the law of conscience, and if he should perish, it would be through unfaithfulness to a law he possessed, not simply because he was not instructed in the plan of God.

23. Can anyone be saved without Christ?

ACTS 4:12_____

24. No man cometh unto the Father but _____.

JOHN 14:6

25. Men are lost because _____

_____. JOHN 3:18

26. They cannot see life because _____

_____. JOHN 3:36

Sometimes nations ignorant of the Word of God come nearer keeping it than some who boast of being Abraham's seed. By *living up* to the light they have, they put to shame those who do not walk in the light they have. However, no pagan morality can satisfy the tests of a holy God. Even the heathen are moral beings, but they do not live up to their own sense of right and wrong. Therefore they can be justly condemned.

Paul now proceeds to prove by three arguments that the heathen have a natural law (2:14-16):

(1) Virtuous acts performed by them (2:14)

(2) The natural operation of conscience (2:15)

(3) Reasonings by which they accuse or excuse one another (2:15)

Dan Crawford, the missionary, said: "The pagans in the heart of Africa are sinning against a flood of light." Charles Scott of China said: "I have never met a heathen living up to his light, and more than that, he knows he is not." Darwin admitted that there was a moral sense in man, even in his worse degradation, an unbridgeable chasm separating him from the animal.

27. Who is ordained to be the Judge of the living and the dead?

ACTS 10:42_____

28. Therefore, in the day of judgment, He will judge the

_____. ACTS 17:31

Righteousness Needed by Sinful Man

(Romans 1:18—3:20) (continued)

Some will ask: "If the heathen have a light to which they are answerable, why not leave them alone?" For the reason that they, like ourselves, allow conscience to be seared, and Satan to have the upper hand. While missionaries find many in heathen lands who are sincerely reaching out after God— bringing the gospel message to them being the answer to that yearning—the vast majority can be aroused to the fact of their lost condition only through the use of the Sword of the Spirit. We ourselves would be heathen had not someone brought us the message of salvation in Christ. The heathen can rise up and condemn us in the judgment if we withhold from them the message committed to us.

Having dealt with the heathen and the moralizer, we turn now to the Jew. The religious Jew might say: "This is not my case." Let us see.

The Jew condemned (Romans 2:17—3:8)

Read ROMANS 2:17-26. Paul faces the Pharisees openly.

1. Is the mere possession of the law of God any protection?

2:17, 18, 25⸺⸺⸺⸺⸺⸺⸺⸺⸺⸺

2. Does the claim of being an instructor in righteousness relieve one?

2:19-21⸺⸺⸺⸺⸺⸺⸺⸺⸺⸺

3. Why is the name of God blasphemed among the heathen?

2:23, 24⸺⸺⸺⸺⸺⸺⸺⸺⸺⸺

4. What kind of circumcision was supposed to go with physical circumcision as a sign of the covenant?

DEUTERONOMY 10:16; 30:6_____

5. What was a frequent charge against Israel?

JEREMIAH 9:26; compare ROMANS 2:25_____

Read ROMANS 2:27-29. One is not saved today because he is orthodox or because he has observed the ordinances. There is always the tendency to substitute the mechanical for the spiritual, the symbol for the reality. Suppose we read verses 28, 29 as follows: "He is not a Christian who is one outwardly, neither is that baptism or communion which is outward; but he is a Christian who is one inwardly, and baptism and communion are those of the heart in the Spirit, not in the letter."

Conclusion: Note that the charges against the Gentile and the Jew are the same.

Gentile

Ungodliness—sins against God (1:21-23)

Intemperance—sins against self (1:21-23)

Unrighteousness—sins against man (1:21-32)

Jew

Ungodliness (2:23)

Intemperance (2:22)

Unrighteousness (2:21)

Paul imagines disputing rabbis raising certain questions. What advantage in being a Jew? Was not Judaism from God? Such questions are here answered.

Read ROMANS 3:1, 2.

6. What is the first great advantage of the Jew?

3:2_____

7. God committed unto us Christians _____

_____. II Corinthians 5:19

What would be the guilt of those to whom the oracles of God were entrusted if they did not walk in the light of their own Scriptures?

Read Romans 3:3, 4.

8. Now another imaginary question from the rabbi: Shall the unbelief of some Jews make God's good faith without effect (3:3)? And Paul answers_____

_____. 3:4a

Read Romans 3:5-8.

Another question from the rabbi: "If our unrighteousness sets off the righteousness of God"—would it be right for God to take vengeance on us (verse 5)? Wouldn't He be unjust in punishing us when His pardon would cause His free grace to stand out by contrast?

9. The answer is_____

_____. 3:6

10. God is going to _____. Psalm 9:8

If God could not righteously punish sin because it would better illustrate His grace not to punish it, then men could sin with impunity (Romans 3:6).

11. If God entertained such a scheme, then why not say (as some already did say untruthfully of apostolic teaching)____

_____. 3:8

There are those today who try to distort the doctrine of free grace, saying that such teaching makes sin safe, especially to the pardoned.

15

12. It is true that where sin abounds _____

_____. ROMANS 5:20

13. But the indwelling Holy Spirit has no part in pious fraud,

He fulfills in the believer _____. ROMANS 8:4

14. Shall we continue in sin that _____

_____. ROMANS 6:1

15. How shall we _____

_____. ROMANS 6:2

The world condemned (Romans 3:9-20)

Read ROMANS 3:9-18.

16. Paul now raises the question: Are we Jews superior? The

answer _____ for all _____. 3:9

He proceeds to bring Old Testament proof—from the Psalms
and the prophets—that Jew and Gentile alike are "guilty
before God" (3:10-18). At least seven things are lacking in
those under sin:

a. Righteousness (3:10)   d. Goodness (3:12)

b. Understanding (3:11)   e. Peace (3:17)

c. Spiritual desire (3:11)   f. Fear of God (3:18)

g. Justification (3:20)

17. The heart _____

_____. JEREMIAH 17:9

This is not popular teaching in these days. The fundamental of present day philosophy is faith in human nature. The Bible teaches that all have a sinful nature, causing evil impulses to express themselves naturally.

Read ROMANS 3:19, 20.

18. What is the great purpose of the law of Moses?

_____ and that all

the world _____. 3:19

19. When one really sees himself in the looking glass of God's law, what will he be apt to say?

JOB 42:6_____

20. Why cannot one arrive at God's righteousness by trying to keep the law?

ROMANS 3:20_____

21. I had not known sin but _____. ROMANS 7:7

The law is the mirror, not the remedy, for the condition it reveals. Stifler says: "As well attempt to cross the ocean on a millstone as to float into heaven on the works of the law."

22. The argument of these verses reverts back to ROMANS

1:17. Therein (in the gospel) is _____

_____

check-up time No. 2

You have now completed your study of the need for righteousness on the part of sinful men, all men without distinction. Review now by rereading the questions and your answers. If you are not sure of an answer, reread the Scripture portion given. Then take the following test to see how well you understand and remember the truths you have studied thus far.

In the right-hand margin write "True" or "False" after each of the following statements.

1. God will visit indignation and wrath upon the unrighteous. _____

2. The heathen, without the Bible, are without excuse. _____

3. When a man lifts his eyes to the skies he should ask himself who created these things. _____

4. The moralizer has no sin of his own to face. _____

5. Salvation by faith encourages loose conduct. _____

6. Some are saved through Christ, others without Him. _____

7. Some day, Christ will judge the world in righteousness. _____

8. Jews were saved because they possessed the law of God. _____

9. The law of Moses was given in order to convict men and women of sin. _____

10. All the world is guilty before God. _____

Turn to page 80 and check your answers.

Righteousness Provided by God
(Romans 3:21—26)

Read ROMANS 3:21, 22.

1. How is it possible to restore guilty man to a righteousness

God can accept?_____

3:22_____

Olhausen calls verses 21, 22 the "citadel of the Christian faith." We might paraphrase it: "Under the gospel a method of justification is revealed, of which God is the Author, and to which all Scriptures bear testimony; that method which, rejecting works of the law as the ground of justification, makes faith in Christ and His merits the only cause, and which extends its benefits to all believers without discrimination" (Bloomfield).

Read ROMANS 3:23, 24. Luther called these verses "the central place of the whole Bible."

2. The first essential of salvation is to recognize that____

_____. 3:23

3. And that justification is *gratis* ("by grace") through

_____. 3:24

One may not be as remote from the righteousness God requires as another, nevertheless he is just as hopeless without Christ. One may stand at the bottom of the deepest mine shaft or on top of the highest mountain. In neither position can he reach the stars.

19

4. There is not _____

_____. ECCLESIASTES 7:20

5. The Scripture has _____ that salvation

might be given to _____. GALATIANS 3:22
Justified means "declared or pronounced righteous"—made as though one had never sinned. This can certainly not be attained through any merit of our own. It must be based on the merits of Another, and placed to our account.

6. It rests on the foundation of the redemption _____

_____. ROMANS 3:24

To be "redeemed" is to be delivered because of a price paid by another.

A. J. Gordon, while traveling on a train, fell into conversation with a fellow passenger on the subject of justification by faith. Said the man to Dr. Gordon: "God deals with *men*, not with a little bit of theological script called faith. When the Almighty admits one to heaven, He will make rigid inquiry about his character, not about his faith" Presently the conductor came along to examine the tickets. When he had passed, Dr. Gordon said: "Did you ever notice how the conductor always looks at the ticket, and takes no pains to inspect the passenger? A railway ticket, if genuine, shows that the person presenting it has complied with the company's conditions and is entitled to transportation. Faith alone entitles a man to that saving grace that is able to produce a character well-pleasing to God, but without faith it is impossible to please God."

Read ROMANS 3:25, 26.

7. The redemption price is now stated—Christ whom God

set forth to be _____. 3:25

Propitiation is one of the great Bible words, meaning "the putting away of wrath." This is required because God is bound to maintain His righteousness. And it is provided because He is love.

8. God commended His love toward us _____

_____. ROMANS 5:8

9. It becomes ours through faith in _____. 3:25

Note that the blood stands for sacrificial death. We could not be saved through faith in Christ's consecrated life. He became our Saviour by means of His atoning death—nothing short of that.

10. This is the fact set forth in the blood sacrifices of the old

covenant, but it was not possible that _____

_____. HEBREWS 10:3, 4

11. Through the death of Christ as an atoning sacrifice, a

way was provided whereby God could be just, yet _____

_____. ROMANS 3:26

12. At the cross of Calvary, mercy and truth _____

and righteousness and peace _____. PSALM 85:10

Righteousness Received by Faith

(Romans 3:27—4:25)

Read ROMANS 3:27-31.

1. Have we any basis for boasting?

3:27_____

2. Our only chance to glory is through_____.

ROMANS 15:17. God forbid _____save in

_____. GALATIANS 6:14

Ruskin: "I believe that the root of every heresy from which the Church has suffered has been the effort of men to *earn* rather than *receive* salvation."

3. Therefore we conclude _____

_____. ROMANS 3:28

4. Do we open the door to moral license (or make void the law) by making salvation by grace rather than through the works of the law?

3:31_____

The apostle proceeds now to bring out the proofs of the position stated in ROMANS 3:21-31:

   a. Righteousness by faith is witnessed by the law and the prophets (3:21).

   b. By faith boasting is excluded (3:27).

   c. The gospel does not set aside but establishes the law (3:31).

Read ROMANS 4:1-5.

5. Who is first mentioned by Paul in support of his doctrine of righteousness received by faith?

4:1_____

This is significant, for the history of Israel did not begin at Sinai, but with Abraham, with whom God made a covenant of grace. It preceded the Mosaic covenant by centuries. If boasting is excluded, what of Abraham? Did he earn or merit the blessings promised?

6. If Abraham had been justified by works, what could he have done?

4:2_____

Literally, "he would have some grounds for self-congratulation."

7. But what saith the Scripture?

4:3_____

_____

Abraham did the most righteous thing possible: he took God at His word. Therefore righteousness was "counted unto him." This is a metaphor from accounting—something put to a man's credit. The word is used eleven times in the context.

8. Did Abraham's faith extend in a sense to Christ?

JOHN 8:56_____

9. What is the one thing that God accepts in exchange for the gift of eternal life?

ROMANS 4:5_____

10. Is even this faith entirely of ourselves?

EPHESIANS 2:8_____

11. What (or who) is the righteousness God will accept to settle accounts?

I CORINTHIANS 1:30 _____

12. Does a Christian *work to be saved,* or *because he is saved?*

TITUS 3:5, 8_____

13. Is saving faith the equivalent of divine righteousness, or is it *counted* so because it is *backed* by sufficient righteousness?

ROMANS 4:5_____

Christ alone is the ground of our righteousness before God. Faith is the channel of receiving it. The infinite worth of saving faith lies in its Object.

Read ROMANS 4:6-8.

14. Who is next used as an illustration of imputed righteousness?

4:6_____

This reference to PSALM 32 is especially to the point, for it is the statement of one who had been taken in great sin (II SAMUEL 12:1-14). He found justification after that experience.

15. What was David's mental state before he became right with God?

PSALM 32:3, 4_____

16. What was his only way out?

PSALM 32:5_____

17. When he turned from his ruined self to God, what happened?

PSALM 32:5-7_____

18. What was the transaction on God's part, in answer to David's faith?

ROMANS 4:7_____

19. Can one who stands in the righteousness of Christ have his sins imputed to him?

4:8; compare JOHN 5:24_____

Paul has already proved that righteousness by faith is witnessed by the law and the prophets (ROMANS 3:21).

Read ROMANS 4:9-12.

20. Was this justification to be for Jews only?

3:29, 30_____

21. Was Abraham justified before his circumcision as a Hebrew or afterward?

4:10_____

Compare GENESIS 15 and 17—the latter, fourteen years later.

22. Did Abraham then receive God's righteousness because he was a Hebrew or through faith as any ordinary individual?

ROMANS 4:11_____

23. What was circumcision in relation to the spiritual experience?

4:11_____

Any ordinance is but a seal or profession of an experience, not a source of salvation. In no age do rites bestow anything. A seal is worthless apart from the matter it attests.

24. How wide was God's purpose—only the salvation of the Jews?

4:12_____

Read ROMANS 4:13-16.

25. Was the promise of blessing to Abraham's descendants based on works of the law?

4:13_____

26. What purpose must the law serve?

4:15_____

27. Therefore salvation is by faith that _____

_____ to the end that _____. 4:16

28. The true descendants of Abraham are those _____

_____. GALATIANS 3:7

Read ROMANS 4:17-22.

29. Abraham was the spiritual father of _____. 4:17

30. Although from the standpoint of nature everything seemed against Abraham and the fulfillment of God's promise of a son, what did he do?

4:18_____

Weymouth gives the last section of 4:18—"Who under utterly hopeless circumstances hopefully believed."

31. Abraham considered not the impotence of his own body

or _____. 4:19

Against all natural appearances, he believed God. This is faith—not blindly trying to think down certain facts or to concentrate on certain desired ends.

32. He put his faith in _____ and gave

_____. 4:20

Personal trust in the divine Promiser, looking wholly away from self, with complete submission and confidence—this is faith.

33. On this basis, Abraham's faith was _____

_____. 4:22

Read ROMANS 4:23-25.

34. In whom are we required to place our faith if we are to receive justifying righteousness?

4:24_____

35. Abraham believed that what God promised He _____

_____ (4:21), and we believe on Him who *has* performed. 4:24

36. This remission of our sins was accomplished by what two things?

4:25 _____ and _____

_____

37. Without the resurrection of Jesus, could we know that Christ's death had any bearing upon the remission of our sins?

4:25; compare I CORINTHIANS 15:17 _____

38. Without His resurrection, we would have no Intercessor at _____. ROMANS 8:33, 34

39. Seeing then that we have _____

_____. HEBREWS 4:14

27

40. Let us therefore _____

_____

_____. HEBREWS 4:14-16

check-up time No. 3

Review now the questions and answers for this section as you have previously done. Then take the following "true" or "false" test as before.

1. The righteousness God provides He gives to those who do their best. _____

2. All have sinned, and come short of the glory of God. _____

3. Our redemption is in Christ Jesus. _____

4. The redemption price is the blood of Christ. _____

5. The blood of bulls and goats took away sin. _____

6. David is the first person Paul mentions to support the teaching of righteousness by faith. _____

7. Abraham was justified by faith. _____

8. Christ Jesus is made unto us righteousness. _____

9. A Christian works diligently to be saved. _____

10. Abraham staggered at the promise of God through unbelief. _____

Turn to page 80 and check your answers.

28

Righteousness Experienced in the Soul
(Romans 5:1—8:17)

We have seen that faith brings justification. We next find what justification brings—peace of mind and heart. Through the work of Christ, accepted by the believer, there comes triumph in the life, even in the midst of trials.

Read ROMANS 5:1-5.

1. Being justified by faith we have _____

_____. 5:1

Peace with God means cessation of hostility between the soul and God. It is something more than a mental sensation or tranquillity of mind. Conscience is at rest.

2. Not only are we saved by grace, but in grace we _____
_____ and rejoice in_____. 5:2

In ROMANS 5:3-5 we have the genealogy of hope—one grace begets another. The rejoicing mentioned is not merely for the future, but it is rejoicing in present grace. Afflictions cannot dampen this hope.

3. We can glory _____. 5:3
The word for *tribulations* means simply, our "troubles."

4. When Peter and others were persecuted for Christ's sake, they were able to _____. ACTS 5:41

5. Hope maketh not _____. ROMANS 5:5
The word is better rendered "put to shame."

6. The certainty of our hope being realized is deepened by the fact that the Holy Spirit sheds abroad in our hearts the

_____. 5:5

Read ROMANS 5:6-11, an expanding of the words, "love of God."

7. God first revealed this love in that _____

_____. 5:6

8. From a human viewpoint, why did it seem unreasonable that God should send His holy Son to die for us?

5:7_____.

By way of illustration Paul contrasts an upright man with a kind man. The latter awakens the special admiration of others, and some would rather risk their lives for a man of this type than for one who was legally good.

9. But God commendeth *His* love toward us in that _____

_____. 5:8

10. Greater love hath no man than this: _____

_____. JOHN 15:13

11. If God had such love for His enemies, what will He surely do for those who have become His children?

ROMANS 5:9_____

12. Much more being reconciled, we _____

_____. 5:10

13. Is it possible to receive salvation through the life of Christ apart from reconciliation through His death?

5:10_____

14. What comes through this knowledge that we are reconciled by His death and kept safe by His life?

5:11_____

15. We rejoice in _____(5:2), we glory in

_____ (5:3) and joy in _____ 5:11

Read ROMANS 5:12-14.

The apostle goes on now to explain the sin principle in man which brings the sentence of God on every human being. Verse 12 is the transition point from the subject of justification by faith to that of victory through yieldedness (chapters 6—8).

16. Over against the fact of God's love, we have the fact that

death passed upon _____ for _____. 5:12

17. The wages of sin is _____. ROMANS 6:23

18. Even before the giving of the moral code, death reigned

even over those _____. 5:14

Since the Fall, death has been universal, even over those not conscious of transgression, such as babies and persons not mentally accountable. This proves that the seeds of sin are at work in all.

Read ROMANS 5:15-19.

19. "But shall not as the offense, so also be the free gift?" (5:15, literally). Will there not be a correspondence between the fall of Adam and the free gift of Christ? The answer is:

"Much more _____." 5:15

Christ's death is not only a reversal of the previous ruin for those who receive Him, but exaltation to heaven with Him forever. Adam, without sin, might have lived on in an unappreciated Eden; but the sinner saved by grace goes to glory singing the praises of the Lamb.

20. ROMANS 5:16 (literally): "The gift exceeds the ruin brought by one." All connected with the Last Adam, having received both grace and righteousness, shall _____

_____. 5:17

21. By the obedience of Christ unto death, who will be made righteous?_____(5:19); those who receive_____

_____. 5:17

The question is often raised: Why should we be involved in Adam's sentence? We had our trial in Adam. We would have done the same had we been in his place. We prove this all our lives. Further, we were in Adam when he sinned.

Read ROMANS 5:20, 21.

The law entered to bring out the fact that, not only are we guilty in Adam, but we are personally sinful. We will be judged, not for Adam's sins, but for our own .

22. The law entered that_____but where sin abounded_____. 5:20

23. Sin has brought the reign of death, but grace reigns_____

_____ 5:21

Some will be saying: "If justification is by faith, then one may live on in sin and still be in divine favor." Paul now proceeds to show that the gospel which justifies by faith without merit is at the same time the power of God which produces a new life within. Sanctification is the result of justification, not its cause.

Read ROMANS 6:1, 2.

24. Shall we continue in sin that grace may be abound? 6:2—

_____

25. Use not your liberty for _____. GALATIANS 5:13

32

26. We are dead to the law that we _____.

GALATIANS 2:19

27. Being dead to sins we should _____

I PETER 2:24

Read ROMANS 6:3-6.

28. Salvation is described as being baptized into_____ signifying identification with Him in His_____. 6:3

29. Burial is the strongest expression of death. We need to see ourselves_____with Him, meaning that the body of sin is _____. 6:6

30. After seeing ourselves buried with Him, we need to see ourselves _____ from the dead by_____

_____. 6:4

31. If we have really experienced death with Christ, we shall also _____. 6:8

32. The rite of water baptism pictures one as _____ and also _____

_____. COLOSSIANS 2:12

Note: Those who do not accept immersion as the New Testament form of baptism will disagree with this interpretation. The author, however, holds that baptism looks back to the cross and the resurrection, and sets forth in a figure death and resurrection with Christ. We reckon on the efficacy of Christ's death for the guilty past, but we are not to stop there. We are also to reckon on the power of His resurrection for the unholy present. That resurrection power is available.

33. If ye then be risen with Christ _____

_____. COLOSSIANS 3:1

34. For ye are dead and _____.
COLOSSIANS 3:3

35. If we have been planted together in the likeness of His
death, we should also bear_____. ROMANS 6:5

36. If the body of sin has been destroyed (literally, "reduced
to a state of inaction") henceforth we will_____. 6:6

Two reckonings

Read ROMANS 6:7-10. As Christ died unto sin and now lives
unto God, so should we.

Read ROMANS 6:11-13.

37. Since legally this is true, the believer is to reckon_____

_____ and _____ through _____

_____. 6:11

In these verses we have the secret of the victorious life. The
first step is to "reckon," or count on certain things as true.
Christ has suffered for my sins. I am therefore bought with
a price and no longer my own. I am *His*, therefore I do not
recognize the old man which is crucified with Him (I CORIN-
THIANS 6:19, 20). Taking this attitude has much to do with
putting Satan to flight. He who thus reckons, finds the Holy
Spirit coming to his assistance.

38. Do not forget there is a double reckoning to do. Reckon

yourselves _____ and reckon yourselves _____

_____. ROMANS 6:11

39. The first is your "amen" to Christ's death for you and your death with Him. The second is counting on the fact of a living Saviour who has _____

_____. MATTHEW 28:18

Two yieldings

40. Having noticed the double "reckoning," we now find a double "yielding."

Yield_____unto God as_____

and_____as_____. ROMANS 6:13

First the inner life, then the members. It is of little use giving God some of our members when the heart is not yielded.

Two negatives

41. Notice also the two negatives here: Let not sin_____

_____(6:12). Neither_____

_____. 6:13

The real seat of sin is in the will. The will makes the members instruments. Sin "reigns" when the will says "yes" to temptation. The Holy Spirit reigns when the will says "no."

Read ROMANS 6:14-17.

42. Does freedom from bondage to the law mean that we are free to sin?

6:15_____

Paul now shows what being free from the law does *not* mean. In ROMANS 7 he shows what it *does* mean to the Jew. In chapter 8 he shows what being under grace means.

43. If one has the new nature through grace, his heart desire

will be to obey_____. 6:17

The word translated "form" means "mold" — and the believer is one whose life is shaped by a mold. Some speak of holding certain doctrines. Paul speaks of doctrine that holds us. When the truth of free and complete salvation lays hold of one, it will shape his thoughts, affections and will after the pattern of Christ.

44. It brings into captivity_____

_____. II CORINTHIANS 10:5

Read ROMANS 6:18, 19.

45. As a result of the transaction with Christ, to what new ownership are we handed over?

6:18_____

46. Does the fact that we have been set free from the dominion of sin imply sinless perfection?

I JOHN 1:8_____

Read ROMANS 6:20-23.

47. If we have truly become servants to God, we will have_____

_____. 6:22

The apostle now returns to remind us once more that salvation is a gift wholly apart from merit (6:23). For the works of sin one draws "wages," but the works of righteousness are not the procuring cause of life. This is a *gift*.

Righteousness Experienced in the Soul

(Romans 5:1—8:17) (continued)

Chapter 7 describes the vain effort of a justified man to attain to sanctification by means of putting himself back under the law which had failed to justify him.

Read ROMANS 7:1-7.

1. First note that sin shall not_____

_____. ROMANS 6:14

In chapter 7, Paul addresses those who know the law, primarily Jewish Christians but including Gentile believers as well. How does he address them?

2. "Know ye not, _____

_____." 7:1

3. "Wherefore, my_____

_____." 7:4

In ROMANS 7:2, 3 Paul illustrates this truth by the case of a married woman, who as long as her husband lives is bound to him, but who when he dies is released from any obligation to him and is free to marry another.

4. "If the husband be dead, she is loosed from_____

_____." 7:2

In verses 2 and 3, the husband dies, leaving the wife free. In verse 4, the wife or widow is looked upon as dead to her husband.

5. "Ye also are become_____by the body of

_____; that ye should be married to_____"
(the risen Christ). 7:4

6. What gave sin its strength? "The strength of sin is_____

_____." I CORINTHIANS 15:56

7. "Is the law sin?"

ROMANS 7:7_____

Read ROMANS 7:8-11.

Paul says he was alive once apart from the law. This seems to have been when he was first saved. Then he put himself back under the law for deliverance from the power of sin. It failed. He "died" all over again.

8. "Sin, taking occasion by the commandment, _____

and by it_____." 7:11

Read ROMANS 7:12-15.

9. The primary purpose of the law was to make sin appear

as_____ that sin by the commandment might become

_____. 7:13

10. In spite of all his efforts to keep the law, Paul found that

he was_____. 7:14

11. He found himself doing_____and failing

to do_____. 7:15

Read ROMANS 7:16-22.

Notice that the pronoun "I" occurs twenty-six times in verses 15-25. There is no mention of the Holy Spirit until we get into chapter 8 where He is mentioned nineteen times. In chapter 7 the law is mentioned very frequently, but only a few times in chapter 8. Paul was showing his wretched thralldom under the law. In spite of his consent to it and his desire to keep it, the sinful nature within was continually overcoming the desire of his mind. How could the *mind* get free from the dictation of the *flesh* so it could have power to do what it really desired to do? The law gave no way out.

12. When one is born of the Spirit, it is God_____
_____. PHILIPPIANS 2:13

13. He works in you_____
_____. HEBREWS 13:21

14. But under the law Paul, apart from the Spirit, found he had the will to do right but_____.
ROMANS 7:18

15. When he would do good_____. 7:21

Read ROMANS 7:23-25.

16. Paul, the Jew, under the law and apart from the Spirit, could only cry out_____ _____
_____. 7:24

17. He had been brought into captivity to_____. 7:23

18. The only way out of this bondage therefore was God through_____. 7:25

Chapter 8 tells of the seven-fold victory Paul found in accepting Jesus Christ.

   a. Over the condemnation of sin (8:1)
   b. Over the dominion of sin (8:2-4)
   c. Over the carnal mind (8:5-10)
   d. Over the mortal body (8:11-13)
   e. Over the bondage of fear (8:14-16)
   f. Over suffering and infirmity (8:17-28)
   g. Over all spiritual foes (8:29-39)

No condemnation (8:1)   No fear (8:15)
No bondage (8:2)   No accusation (8:33)
No debt (8:12)   No separation (8:35)
No corruption (8:21)

19. Paul is still developing the statement of ROMANS 6:14—

Sin shall _____.

He has answered about the law. Only through spiritual union with Christ is there hope.

Read ROMANS 8:1-4.

20. In Christ one is freed from _____

_____. 8:1

(Literally, "judgment"; same word in JOHN 5:24)

21. He shall not come_____but is passed

_____. JOHN 5:24

The last ten words of ROMANS 8:1 do not belong in the text. The A.S.V. omits them. They belong, however, in verse 4.

In ROMANS 8:1 it is not a question of the believer's heart condemning him. We will always find things in us worthy of condemnation. Romans 8:1 has to do with the believer's *standing*, which is complete because it rests wholly on Christ.

22. But what of the sins a Christian commits? "If we confess

_____."

I JOHN 1:9

As to fellowship with the Father and the sense of pardon, confession is the only course. If there is not confession, then there is the rod of correction (I CORINTHIANS 11:32).

23. The dominion of the law of sin has been broken and the believer has now been brought under the law of the Spirit of

life in Christ Jesus. This law has made me_____.

ROMANS 8:2

24. Through the work of the incarnate Son of God, the power of sin for the believer has been broken that_____ _____might be fulfilled in us who walk after_____. 8:4

The Holy Spirit is ready to take over—and lives the Christ-life in us.

25. As we yield to the Holy Spirit, we can say: It is not I who lives but_____. GALATIANS 2:20

Read ROMANS 8:5-8.

26. Humanity is divided into two classes: They that are after_____and they_____ _____. 8:5

27. To be carnally minded is_____(literally "the mind of the flesh"), becasue the carnal mind is not____ _____neither_____. 8:7

28. Those who "mind . . . the flesh" cannot_____. 8:8

The carnal man is an unspiritual Christian, one not yielded to the Holy Spirit (I CORINTHIANS 3:1-3).

Read ROMANS 8:9-13.

29. The Holy Spirit is called the Spirit _____ and the Spirit of _____. 8:9

This shows Paul's view of the divine majesty of the Son. The Holy Spirit is the Revealer of Christ to the soul (JOHN 16:13, 14).

30. As the result of our connection with a sinful race the seeds

of death are in_____but the Spirit gives us_____

because of_____(ROMANS 8:10)—the righteousness of God in Christ wherein we stand.

The believer's body may be subject to death, but through regeneration, he is certain to be rescued from the "second death."

31. The same power of the Spirit that raised Jesus from the

dead will_____. 8:11

The indwelling presence of the Holy Spirit now is the guarantee of future resurrection of the body.

32. Our great debt is not to the flesh, but to the Spirit. Hence,

the control of the old nature in us must be through_____.
8:12, 13

The apostle foresaw how many would try to mortify the self-life in ways that would only pamper it and minister to its pride. Victory comes through a daily yielding to the Holy Spirit who is able to change our desires.

Read ROMANS 8:14-17.

33. To have the leading of the Holy Spirit is an evidence that

one is a _____. 8:14

34. If one has come to know God as his Father, he will not

live in fear of the law, but will have the_____

whereby_____. 8:15

35. We can know here and now that we are God's children

because_____

_____

_____. 8:16

The expression "Abba, Father" in 8:15 is half Hebrew (or Syriac) and half Greek. Perhaps Paul used both these words for "papa" because to him it typified the fusion of Jew and Gentile in Christ.

36. When we become God's children we are heirs_____

and_____. 8:17

37. What is one way whereby we may know whether or not we are really His?

8:17_____

Righteousness Guaranteed a Permanent Blessing
(Romans 8:18—39)

Read ROMANS 8:18-25.

1. Whatever we are called upon to endure as a Christian, we will remember that it is not_____

_____. 8:18

2. All creation that is under the curse awaits_____

_____. 8:19

3. This looks to the day when_____

_____and we shall then_____. COLOSSIANS 3:4

4. The deliverance of all creation will be associated with the believer's deliverance from_____. ROMANS 8:21

5. Earth is at present but a swinging cemetery. It echoes with the groans of many creatures, and while even Christians groan within themselves now, what do they anticipate?

8:23_____

6. The indwelling Holy Spirit is the earnest of our inheritance until_____. EPHESIANS 1:13, 14

7. When our Lord returns He will change the bodies of our humiliation that they may be fashioned like_____.
PHILIPPIANS 3:21

Read ROMANS 8:26, 27. The Spirit *also* (in addition to His other work mentioned) helps our infirmities in prayer.

8. We know not_____. 8:26

9. What does the Holy Spirit do for us?

8:26_____

_____

10. His intercession for us is according to_____.
                                                    8:27

11. Did Paul himself always know just how to pray?

II CORINTHIANS 12:8, 9_____

12. If we are to receive just what we ask for, we must pray as Christ did, according_____. MARK 14:36

Read ROMANS 8:28-30.

13. In God's dealings with His own children, how many things does He work together for good?

8:28_____

Since this is true, one who is in His will need not_____.

                                                    PSALM 46:2

14. Even though taken by death, we have_____

_____. II CORINTHIANS 5:1

15. In all these trials, to what is God seeking to conform His child?

ROMANS 8:29_____

16. Did God foreknow *all* that was coming to us before we were born?

ISAIAH 46:9, 10_____

45

17. When He chose us in Christ before the foundation of the world, it was that_____

_____. EPHESIANS 1:4

18. What comes before God's predestination?

ROMANS 8:29; compare I PETER 1:2_____

Foreknowledge no more determines facts than after-knowledge. The omniscient God is able to know in advance what course will be chosen by every individual. He therefore knew who every one of His children would be, and these are the "elect." Outside heaven's gate we may read: "Whosoever will may enter." On the inside of the gate we might read: "Those who would enter were foreknown and already listed here."

19. It follows that since the saints are foreknown and predestined they are also

a. _____

b. _____

c. _____. ROMANS 8:30

Here is the great comfort of those in affliction. The past tense is here used with wonderful power of something yet future to us—glorification. So unbreakable is this chain, that the last link is viewed as accomplished already. If we have the witness of the Spirit that we are children of God, we can consider ourselves as good as already in heaven—as much so as though we had already been there a million years.

20. Already He has_____

_____.

EPHESIANS 2:6

21. That in the ages to come_____

_____. EPHESIANS 2:7

46

Note: There is not a word of Scripture to suggest that any person is foreordained to be lost. Those who imagine themselves excluded from salvation because of the foreknowledge of God are deceiving themselves. Whosoever *will* may come.

Read ROMANS 8:31-34. Summing up, Paul shows now the absolute security of all those in the purpose of God.

22. If God be for us, who_____? 8:31

23. If Christ is for us at the right hand of the throne of God, who is he that condemneth?

8:34_____

24. Jesus said it was the Father's will that of all the Father had given Him, He should_____

_____. JOHN 6:39

25. Who would like to lay charges against us?

REVELATION 12:9, 10_____

26. Why can't he make his charges stick? The blood of Jesus

Christ_____ (I JOHN 1:7)

and we have an_____. I JOHN 2:1

27. Though a Christian may backslide and suffer loss, he shall

not be utterly cast down, for_____

_____. PSALM 37:23, 24

28. The solid basis of our justification is that Christ_____

and_____ and_____,

ROMANS 8:34

Read ROMANS 8:35-39.

29. Who can separate us from God's love in Christ?

8:38, 39_____

47

The original for *creature* is "created thing." *Nothing* can separate the child of God from Him.

30. There is no separation from the love of _____ (8:35), or from the love of _____. 8:39

31. Therefore we are _____ through _____. 8:37

check-up time No. 4

Review now as you have done previously. Then take the following "true" or "false" test as before.

1. Romans 5 indicates the first thing justification brings is peace. _____

2. It was for the ungodly Christ died. _____

3. Baptism into Jesus Christ means baptism into His death. _____

4. Sin must inevitably have dominion over us. _____

5. The law of the Spirit of life in Christ sets the believer free from the law of sin and death. _____

6. Believers are delivered from condemnation. _____

7. The "adoption" for which believers now wait is the redemption of the soul. _____

8. God has predestinated believers to be conformed to the image of His Son. _____

9. In addition to predestinating and calling believers, He has also, according to Romans 8:30, condemned them. _____

10. God justifies the believer for whom Christ died. _____

Turn to page 80 and check your answers.

Righteousness Rejected by Jews
(Romans 9—11)

A large section is now given to the case of Israel. At the time this epistle was written, the Church was comprised largely of Jewish believers. There were difficulties to be cleared up. One serious problem for the Jew was: How could God reject His chosen people?

Read ROMANS 9:1-5.

How did Paul sometimes feel in his great burden for the souls of his fellow Jews? Someone has described his feeling as a "spark from the fire of Christ's substitutionary love."

1. What made their rejection of their Messiah so sad?

To them pertained_____

_____

_____. 9:4

2. Was Christ, on the fleshward side, a Jew?

9:5; compare JOHN 4:9_____

3. What dignity did Paul ascribe to the Messiah?

ROMANS 9:5_____

4. What did Paul mean by the "adoption" of Israel?

EXODUS 4:22; HOSEA 11:1_____

5. What did he mean by the "glory"?

EXODUS 40:34, 35_____

49

6. What did he mean by the "law" committed to them?

DEUTERONOMY 4:8_____

Read ROMANS 9:6-13. Theme: The Jews have failed; God has not.

7. What distinction did God make concerning Israel from the outset?

9:6_____

The promises to Israel were not based on mere physical descent. They were also dependent on spiritual factors. God could still make the same distinction, receiving certain ones because of faith and rejecting others because of unbelief.

Paul proceeds to show that even within the circle of promise (to Abraham), there was still an election (9:7-11).

8. Were all Israelites saved because they were the physical seed of Abraham?

9:7_____

Hagar's son was the seed of Abraham, but not in the intention of promise (see GENESIS 18:10). Jacob was chosen; Esau was rejected (9:13).

Read ROMANS 9:14-17.

9. If Jacob was chosen, it was not on his merits. If Esau was rejected, was God unrighteous?

9:14_____

10. If we do not understand His acts, what should we remember?

ISAIAH 55:8_____

_____

For as the heavens_____

_____.

ISAIAH 55:9

50

11. The omniscient God may have mercy on_____.

ROMANS 9:15

12. Even if we accept His salvation, it is God who_____

_____.PHILIPPIANS 2:13

Paul illustrates in ROMANS 9:17 by showing God's side of Pharaoh's case. On one hand was a man battling against right and bringing ruin on his own head. On the other hand was God, making Pharaoh a monument of judgment. God hardened his heart by sentencing him to have his own way.

Read ROMANS 9:18-21.

13. Whom He will He hardeneth (9:18). Does God harden those whose desire is toward Him, or those opposed to Him?

II THESSALONIANS 2:10, 11_____

Dr. W. H. Griffith-Thomas: "Hardening of heart is a process by which the almighty power of God deals with a creature who rejects His will."

14. Is it of any use to argue with God who knows the thoughts and intents of man's heart?

ROMANS 9:19, 20_____

15. If the potter throws out a complete vessel, is it not likely that there is a sufficient reason?

9:21 _____

It is not implied that the potter makes a vessel on purpose to destroy it.

Read ROMANS 9:22, 23.

16. Are all men fitted for glory?

9:22 _____

17. What is God's feeling toward those fitted for destruction?

9:22 _____

_____

The preparation of the saved for glory is everywhere (9:23) ascribed to God.

18. Note the contrast: The kingdom is prepared for the____

____MATTHEW 25:33, 34), but everlasting fire for the____

_____. MATTHEW 25:33, 41

Read ROMANS 9:24-29.

19. Paul here shows that God has always had a people where some religious folks did not suspect. His true children are not always where the biggest noise is going on. What then about the Gentiles, whom the Jewish leaders regarded as

fitted only to destruction? Some Gentiles God has_____

_____. 9:24

Read ROMANS 9:30-33.

20. How have certain of the Gentiles found righteousness?

Of (or, by)_____. 9:30

21. What had happened to many religious Jews who had reasoned that all Jews must be saved because descended from Abraham?

9:31 _____

22. Why had they missed the possession of salvation?

9:32 _____

23. What had the prophets foreseen concerning Israel?

That a stumbling block would be laid in_____. 9:33

The Gentiles did not pursue righteousness, yet overtook it by confessing themselves lost and receiving the Saviour. Many Jews pursued it in the wrong way and lost it altogether, thinking to claim it on their own merits.

The closing thought of chapter 9—"They [Israel] stumbled at that stumblingstone [that is, Christ]" (9:32).

24. They failed to attain standing with God because they sought it not_____.9:32

In chapter 10 the apostle proceeds to show how they sought it—through their own religiousness and earnestness. There was no withholding of divine grace; it was their own unwillingness to receive God's plan of salvation.

Read ROMANS 10:1-4.

25. The heart desire of Paul was that_____.

10:1

26. He gives them credit for_____but it was not_____

_____(10:2). Or, "They have a zeal for God but not an intelligent one."

A locomotive has enormous powers of usefulness as long as it is run on the track, otherwise great destruction results. Religious zeal is worthless unless it is run on the track of God's laying.

27. Of what were these Jews ignorant?

10:3 _____

And what were they trying to do?

10:3 _____

28. What is God's estimate of human righteousness, however good?

ISAIAH 64:6_____

A man's own virtues often look so great to him that he fails to see his need of salvation (ROMANS 3:23). Rittenhouse, the astronomer, found a piece of silk thread on the great lens of his telescope, which caused the stars to be obscured. Even a piece of fiber can do the same. A great planet hidden behind a speck held near the eye! Men allow a speck of self-righteousness to hide from them the Sun of righteousness, the Light of the world.

29. Righteousness that can give one standing with God is to to be found only in_____. 10:4

Read ROMANS 10:5-8.

30. The righteousness of the law required_____ the things written therein. 10:5

31. This is in contrast with the righteousness which is of

_____. 10:6

32. Faith's righteousness does not stop to ask such questions

as _____? (10:6) or_____

_____? 10:7

These are proverbial expressions indicating something impossible (compare PROVERBS 30:4; PSALM 139:7-10). Paul adapts this quotation to its ultimate and deepest sense. God's plan does not require us to do something beyond reach of accomplishment, or even to explain what we cannot understand. We do not have to explain the incarnation or the resurrection—only believe and we shall get the evidence in our own souls. God's way is so simple that the Jews wouldn't take it.

33. The word of truth_____even in_____

_____the word of_____. ROMANS 10:8

54

Read ROMANS 10:9-11.

34. We are called upon to confess Jesus as_____and

to believe in the heart that_____.
                                                    10:9

35. Concerning Jesus it is essential to believe that He is____

_____(JOHN 20:31) and that God_____

_____. ROMANS 10:9

36. Why is belief in His resurrection essential?

Thus He was_____. ROMANS 1:4

37. He was crucified for_____and raised for_____

_____. ROMANS 4:25

38. With the heart we_____but with the mouth___

_____. ROMANS 10:10

39. "I believed, therefore_____." PSALM 116:10

40. Out of the abundance_____the mouth_____.
                                                    LUKE 6:45

41. They overcame the devil by the blood of the Lamb and by

_____. REVELATION 12:11

Read ROMANS 10:12, 13.

42. Is there any distinction between Jew and Gentile as to
human sinfulness before God?

ROMANS 3:22, 23_____

43. Is there distinction in the wealth of God's grace to those
who want to be saved, Jew or Gentile?

10:12 _____

44. What is God's inclusive word that proves that He has nothing to do with distinctions between Jew and Gentile?

10:13 _____

John Berridge wrote: "I am so glad it says 'whosoever' instead of 'John Berridge,' for there might be another John Berridge; but when I read 'whosoever,' I know it means me."

Read ROMANS 10:14-21. We now have an argument for the evangelization of the heathen, versus the jealous reserve of Judaism.

45. Since we found the joy of salvation through the witness of someone else, can we expect others to be saved unless we also witness?

10:14 _____

46. Can we expect that our witness for Christ will always be welcomed?

10:16 _____

47. Nevertheless what is *God* saying about those who witness for the gospel?

10:15 _____

_____

48. What did Jesus say His witnesses might expect in many cases from men?

JOHN 15:18-21_____

49. When presenting the gospel to others, what must we always remember?

ROMANS 10:17_____

50. What was the tragic thing about God's invitation to His people Israel?

10:21 _____

Righteousness Rejected by Jews

(Romans 9—11) (continued)

What would the Jew now say to the teaching that the promise of God was to all men without distinction? What of the many Old Testament promises having to do with Israel's national blessing? These could not be realized in the Church. Here is a chapter that should warn us against the spiritualizing methods employed by some teachers today. Are saved Gentiles the so-called "spiritual Israel" and "true Jews"? Is the "house of Israel" now "the house of God," the Church? Are saved Gentiles the "seed of Jacob" and the "seed of Abraham"?

Read ROMANS 11:1-7.

1. Is God now through with Israel as a people?

11:1 _____

2. Has God cast away Israel?

11:2 _____

3. Though at many periods individual Israelites forfeited the promised blessings, what has always been true?

11:4 _____

4. And what is also true in this age?

11:5 _____

5. What do you think of the teaching of some today that there is no such thing as a genuine Jewish Christian?

11:7 _____

Read ROMANS 11:8-10.

6. What is the trouble with Jews who refuse Jesus, after having Him fairly presented to them?

11:8 _____

7. When God says: "Let their eyes be darkened that they may not see," does it mean that He makes them helpless victims of an arbitrary sentence, or is this blinding the result of their own persistent unbelief?

ISAIAH 29:10-13_____

8. Why was it necessary for God to take away from some in Israel the power of spiritual perception?

JEREMIAH 5:21, 23_____

9. They were blinded because_____.
EZEKIEL 12:2

10. While many talk about the blindness of the Jew, what is said concerning the blindness of unbelief in general?

II CORINTHIANS 4:4_____

_____

_____

11. Why will God send strong delusion to thousands of Gentiles as well as Jews?

II THESSALONIANS 2:10, 11_____

_____

Read ROMANS 11:11-16.

12. Are the Jews then hopelessly lost as a nation?

11:11 _____

13. How was God at the time overruling the Jewish rejection of Christ to accomplish His wider purpose?

11:11_____.

14. What will eventually be the reaction of the Jews when they see divine blessing poured out upon believing Gentiles?

11:11, 12_____

15. While Israel as a nation, because of unbelief, is not at present to the forefront in God's purposes, does Paul suggest that they are to have any future place as a people?

11:15 _____

16. When God addressed Israel through Isaiah concerning the last dark days, what did He say would eventually occur?

ISAIAH 60:2_____

_____

17. When national blessing returns to Israel, what will the Gentiles do?

ISAIAH 60:3_____

18. What will the sons of Israel do in these coming days?

ISAIAH 60:4_____

The idea of the "firstfruit" in ROMANS 11:16 is taken from the Old Testament (LEVITICUS 23:10). The firstfruit was the pledge of the balance to come and imparted its consecration to the whole mass. The patriarchs, as consecrated to God, were the pledge of the final consecration of the whole nation and the fulfillment of all the promises in due season. The root of Israel still lives and will not die.

Read ROMANS 11:17-21.

19. If Israel is the olive tree, what are converted Gentiles?

11:17_____grafted in (contrary to nature) among

_____partaking of_____.

To Israel pertained_____

_____

_____. 9:4

Of whom as concerning the flesh_____. 9:5

20. For what reason alone were Jewish branches broken off?

11:20 _____

21. On what ground alone can Gentiles be in the favor of God?

11:20 _____

Therefore, be_____. 11:20

22. Does the Gentile stand in the same peril as the Jew?

11:21 _____

Read ROMANS 11:22-26.

23. If Gentile believers continue in divine favor, it will be

only because they_____; otherwise_____

_____. 11:22

24. On the other hand, if a Jew turns to Christ_____

_____. 11:23

25. Therefore we should remember that we were grafted____

____into_____. 11:24

An objection has been raised by some that the gardener does not graft the wild into the stem already under cultivation, but the reverse. Nevertheless it is claimed that in the East this very thing is sometimes done: the wild grafted into an exhausted tree to revive it. This is the very effect which the apostle here shows. In the end, Israel's tree will be greatly revived.

26. Eventually the natural branches will be_____. 11:24

27. The knowledge of these truths will keep Gentile believers from being_____. 11:25

28. The blindness of Israel is not total, but only____and until _____. 11:25

29. When this "fullness" is attained, and when the Deliverer (Christ) shall come out of Zion, what part of remaining Israel will be saved?

11:26 _____

Read ROMANS 11:27-32.

30. What has God covenanted to do especially for Israel?

11:27 _____

31. Are the promises of God to Israel revoked?

11:29 _____

32. The Jews are yet to_____. 11:31

Read ROMANS 11:33-36.

This is a good place to pause and worship. O the inexhaustible resources of the wisdom and knowledge of God! How unsearchable are His decisions!

check-up time No. 5

Review again as before. Then take the following
"true" or "false" test as previously.

1. By the "glory" in Romans 9:4, Paul meant
the glory of the Lord in the tabernacle. _____

2. The real children of Abraham are all of his
natural descendants. _____

3. All men are fitted for glory. _____

4. The Jews failed to attain standing with God
because they sought it by works of the law _____

5. It was Jeremiah who said all our
righteousnesses are as filthy rags. _____

6. In Romans 10:9-11, Paul says the two things
required for salvation are to repent and confess.

_____

7. The Jewish nation is at present judicially
blinded because of unbelief. _____

8. Gentile unbelievers stand in the same peril
as Jewish unbelievers. _____

9. God had cast away His people Israel. _____

10. Eventually, the natural branches will be
grafted in again. _____

Turn to page 80 and check your answers.

62

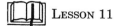

Righteousness Manifested in Daily Life
(Romans 12—16)

"I beseech you therefore . . ." When it comes to inciting believers to greater devotedness to Christ, it is significant that it is by entreaty in view of the salvation and security we have in Christ. This "therefore" links the entire practical appeal to the sublime argument of the previous chapters—salvation by grace from start to finish.

Read ROMANS 12:1, 2.

1. On what ground does Paul make his appeal?

By the_____. 12:1

2. What is to be "presented"?

12:1 _____

(*Presented* is the same word rendered *yield* in chapter 6, meaning "utter abandonment to Him.")

3. Why should we be "living sacrifices"?

12:1 _____

4. What should we consider?

I SAMUEL 12:24_____

The apostle doubtless had the burnt sacrifice in mind in speaking of "living sacrifices." This offering pictures Christ offering Himself to God in perfect devotion to the Father's will (LEVITICUS 1:6-9). The priest or offerer got nothing of this offering. A "living sacrifice," in contrast to the dying sacrifices of the Old Testament, is a life completely dedicated to Him.

5. Be not _____but_____

_____. 12:2

The Greek word for *conformed* is translated in the A.S.V. "be not fashioned." How prone we are to follow the world's fashions! The word for *transformed* means "transfigured."

6. What will we thus prove about the will of God?

12:2 _____

7. If we thus yield, by what power will our minds be renewed?

TITUS 3:5_____

The word used for *renewing* occurs only in these two passages and means "renovating."

Read ROMANS 12:3-8.

8. What does Paul suggest as one of the firstfruits of this consecration?

Not to_____. 12:3

Read ROMANS 12:9, 10.

9. What is the defect in much of the Christian profession of love?

12:9 _____

Dissimulation is "hypocrisy." Is there hypocritical love in the church?

10. When some people speak fair words, what is often to be suspected?

PROVERBS 26:25_____

11. How does Paul stress the fruits of true Christian humility?

ROMANS 12:10_____

The word rendered *preferring* means "anticipating." To anticipate one another is to try to get ahead of the other person in showing kindness—see who can be most courteous, kind and helpful. Christianity is a school of courtesy.

Read ROMANS 12:11-13.

12. What motto do some employers like to stress before their employees?

12:11 _____

The word for *business* in this verse has no commercial element. It refers to spiritual activity, business of God. Christianity is something that has to do with all our business. It *is* the business of our lives.

13. In our business for God, what should be our spirit?

12:11 _____

The word means "boiling hot.'"

14. What will keep us on fire?

Continuing_____. 12:12

The expression is a Greek metaphor from hunting dogs, that never leave the trail until they have their prey.

Read ROMANS 12:14-16.

15. What echo do we have of the Sermon on the Mount?

12:14; compare MATTHEW 5:44_____

16. How will true Christian fellowship express itself?

ROMANS 12:15_____

_____

17. What is the natural relation of one member of the body toward all others?

I CORINTHIANS 12:26_____

18. Is a well-balanced Christian a person who cannot accommodate himself to others?

ROMANS 12:16——————————————————

19. What is most out of place in any Christian?

Being—————————————————————. 12:16

Read ROMANS 12:17-21.

20. What trait should especially stand out in every Christian?

12:17 ——————————————————————

The word for *provide* means "think beforehand." We should constantly study to have all our acts transparent and straightforward, lest our Christian testimony be hindered.

21. Name another trait vital to Christian testimony.

12:18 ——————————————————————

22. Nevertheless, while we are to pursue peace, we are also

to—————————————————————. PSALM 34:14

23. What is one good way to ruin one's Christian testimony?

ROMANS 12:19——————————————————

24. What is always the best solution to the problem of self-defense?

12:19 ——————————————————————

The reference is not to emergencies when life may be imperiled.

> "To be kind to the kind is civility,
> To be unkind to the unkind is heathenism,
> To be unkind to the kind is Satanic,
> To be kind to the unkind is Christianity."

25. What is the surest way to break down enmity in another?

12:20 _____

The words, "heap coals of fire on his head," are given in one translation: "Thou shalt bring him a burning sense of shame."

Believers had thrown off the bondage of legalism. They were taught that Christ had made them free indeed. At that stage of Church history there may have arisen a feeling among some that the heavenly citizenship set them free from man-made decrees. Some might have been tempted to attack the government. Had they embarked on such a program, all would have perished. The apostle gives a much-needed note of caution.

Read ROMANS 13:1-5.

26. How many were to be subject to the authorities?

13:1 _____

27. Is there any human government that is without divine responsibility to rule over its citizens?

13:1 _____

28. Was even the government presided over by Nero in that day authorized by God?

13:1 _____

29. What authority is vested in kings and governors by God?

I PETER 2:13, 14_____

_____

30. Who are declared presumptuous and self-willed?

II PETER 2:10_____

31. Who gave Nebuchadnezzar of Babylon his authority over men?

JEREMIAH 27:6-8_____

32. Who sets up kings and removes them?

DANIEL 2:21_____

33. Who has the final disposition of all political matters?

DANIEL 4:32_____

34. Even though rulers are a scourge to a people, what hand of power must be recognized back of them?

DANIEL 5:18-20_____

Laws and governments are of God. Without them the race would be little better than beasts. The Bible does not prescribe any one particular form of government, but leaves the Christian free to enter as a spirit of good into any form. Where God's Word prevails, hurtful laws and institutions are abolished; for the fundamental of Christianity is living for others and the equality of all men before God. However, God often deals with the sins of a people by giving them hard taskmasters.

35. What is one doing who attempts to use revolutionary action against government?

ROMANS 13:2_____

36. What will such subversive action bring in the end?

_____

(13:2—"judgment")

One may employ action within the limits of the existing constitution, but he will not plot against government nor resist its decrees except when government requires him to do that which God forbids (ACTS 5:29).

68

37. Does civil authority, even in its most distorted form, usually favor wrong as wrong, or oppose right as right?

ROMANS 13:3———————————————————————

Even Nero's persecution of Christians was bolstered by the theory of the preservation of order. God's purpose was served, moreover, in that the blood of the martyrs became the seed of the Church.

38. What can usually be said of the favor or wrath of a ruler?

PROVERBS 14:35————————————————————————

39. What credentials do rulers have from God, regardless of the form of government?

ROMANS 13:4———————————————————————

"Bearing the sword" was a phrase expressing the power of magistrates. The sword was carried before processions and on special occasions. Capital punishment is here sanctioned.

Read ROMANS 13:6, 7.

40. Because of the authority of the government, Christians should also ————————————————————————. 13:6

41. Tax assessors and gatherers are called————————————.
13:6

42. Render therefore to whom they are due (a)——————

(b)——————— (c)——————— (d)——————. 13:7

43. Did Jesus approve paying taxes to support the sustaining of police and soldiers empowered to take life if necessary?

MATTHEW 22:17-21———————————————————

44. Does the New Testament sanction discourtesy toward those in authority?

I PETER 2:17————————————————————————

Read ROMANS 13:8-10.

Turning from the subject of debt to government, the apostle expands the subject: "Be in debt to no man." Some think the reference is primarily to money debts.

45. Should a Christian of all persons have a thought for the interests of a creditor when it is at all possible to pay?

PROVERBS 3:27, 28_____

It is a sad fact that many who make high professions of Christianity are in debt on all hands.

46. Which is the greatest of all debts which probably we will never get paid?

ROMANS 13:8_____

47. What one word sums up the law of God?

GALATIANS 5:14_____

48. Love worketh _____. ROMANS 13:10

MacLaren: "If love to God does not find a field for its manifestation in active love to man, worship in God's house will be a mockery."

Read ROMANS 13:11-14.

49. What one thing was certain as to the time of the Lord's return?

13:11_____

50. How did Paul feel about the darkness of those times?

13:12_____

51. What has from the first been the blessed hope of the Church?

TITUS 2:13_____

Paul hoped for the translation, yet spoke of the possibility of departing to be with the Lord through death.

70

52. What is the only safe course for Christians, since it is not ours to know exactly the times and seasons?

Romans 13:12, 13_____

_____

53. What is the final exhortation?

13:14_____and_____

_____

To "put on the new man" means, briefly, to let the characteristics of Christ in us appear and predominate (Ephesians 4:24-32).

54. The new man is _____

_____. Colossians 3:10

Righteousness Manifested in Daily Life
(Romans 12—16) (continued)

One problem in the early Church was the convert from Judaism or paganism who was full of scruples which, to an enlightened Christian, seemed morbid and foolish. These were a sore trial to many believers who were doubtless inclined to argue with them or pronounce them hopeless fanatics. The apostle rebukes these unduly scrupulous people for their "legalism" and the strong Christians for failure to bear with the weak. Unchristian conduct is often shown in contending over scriptural truth.

Read ROMANS 14:1-3.

1. What is the Christian attitude toward people who seem to entertain unwarranted scruples?

14:1_____

The words "not to doubtful disputations" are better rendered "not to criticisms of his scruples."

2. What was one of the chief matters argued about in the early days?

14:2_____

3. Although we cannot agree with some of the fine distinctions made by others, what is to be remembered, if we know that these persons have accepted Jesus Christ?

14:3_____

Read ROMANS 14:4-6.

4. What shows plainly that the Old Testament sabbath law was not in effect under the gospel?

"Let every _____." 14:5

5. Is the particular day of the week that is kept the essential thing?

14:6_____

6. And as to diet, what is the essential thing?

14:6_____

7. Has any person a right to judge another over a matter of what day of the week is kept unto God?

COLOSSIANS 2:16_____

Some Jewish believers in the early Church still clung to Saturday worship as a permanent moral obligation in addition to the first day or Lord's day. Paul saw no harm, even if they kept every day in the week holy unto the Lord. Those who had the greater light concerning the resurrection day were to bear with them in love. It was not a matter to bar fellowship, so long as they were fully persuaded in their own minds. The same might be said of Seventh Day Adventists of our own day were it not for their acceptance of more serious errors based on alleged revelations to Mrs. Ellen White.

Read ROMANS 14:7-9.

8. Since all believers are bound together in Christ, what is the great fact for us to remember as Christians?

14:7, 8_____

Read ROMANS 14:10-13.

9. As to all differences of opinion, with whom must we all reckon?

14:10_____

10. Is it possible that in that day many will suffer loss who will nevertheless themselves be eternally saved?

I CORINTHIANS 3:15_____

11. Every one of us shall _____

ROMANS 14:12

We need not try to judge others here, since we will not have to there. Each must stand in his own light.

12. In view of accountability for self alone, let us decide this rather:_____

_____

_____. 14:13

Read ROMANS 14:14-19.

13. While the apostle grants that many of the questions of ceremonial uncleanness, days, etc., were trivial, what did he feel as to the danger of tampering with another's conscience?

14:14_____

_____

14. Even though we must give up some things to avoid offending another's conscience, what is more precious than our Christian liberty?

14:15_____

Love enables us to abridge some of our liberties in order to help another who needs more scriptural light. Mistaken conscience calls for correction, but never violation.

15. What is more vital among Christians than discussions about days, meat, drink, etc.?

14:17_____

16. In addition to seeking the Spirit's graces, we should_____

_____. 14:19

Read ROMANS 14:20-23.

17. Why is violation of conscience always dangerous?

14:20_____

18. Although we can do certain things without personal danger, why is it necessary sometimes to forego them?

14:21_____

_____

19. If one does something which causes his conscience uneasiness, what will be the result?

14:23_____

The word for "damned" means "judged" or "condemned."

Many in the church become more zealous for certain doctrines than they are for the fine points of Christian conduct. Zeal for an intellectual knowledge of the Bible is a poor substitute for the high-level, sacrificial Christian life—willingness even to give up lawful things for the sake of influence upon a weaker brother.

ROMANS 15 continues the same subject through verse 7. Read verses 1-7.

20. Whom did Jesus live to please?

JOHN 8:29_____

21. As a part of pleasing God, whom also should we please?

ROMANS 15:1-3_____

22. The Scriptures were written to give us hope. Hence, we are to be likeminded toward whom?

15:4, 5_____

23. The eventual purpose of this is what?

15:6 _____

_____

24. What practical application does this have?

We ought to _____ as _____

_____. 15:7

The rest of chapter 15 deals with the ministry of Christ and that of Paul.

Read ROMANS 15:8-13.

25. The ministry of Jesus Christ was particularly for whom?

15:8 _____

26. Do the Old Testament Scriptures indicate, however, that the mercy of God would ultimately be extended to Gentiles?

15:9-12 _____

27. Believers—Jews or Gentiles—should therefore be filled with _____ and _____ and abound in_____

_____. 15:13

Read ROMANS 15:14-33.

28. Paul was the one chosen to minister the gospel of God on behalf of Jesus Christ to whom?

15:16 _____

29. Paul says he has fully preached the gospel to them from

_____ to _____. 15:19

30. Ultimately, Paul hoped to get as far as _____

(15:24) and on the way stop at _____. 15:28

31. Just now, however, he is headed for _____ to minister to the Jewish saints there. 15:25, 26

32. He is uncertain what reception he will get in Judea from

_____ and in Jerusalem from _____

15:31

ROMANS 16 consists largely of greetings to various believers in Rome.

Read ROMANS 16:1-16.

33. First, he commends to the Roman believers the bearer of this epistle, a sister named _____16:1, 2

34. Who would have given their lives for Paul, if necessary? 16:3, 4_____

35. Who were saved before Paul was? 16:7_____

36. Name three persons in Rome, to whom Paul sends greetings, who were his kinsmen. 16:7, 11_____

37. Whose mother seems to have been a "mother" to Paul? 16:13_____

Read ROMANS 16:17-27.

38. Against whom does Paul warn the Roman Christians?

Those who cause _____ and offenses _____

_____16:17

39. Who are these people actually serving? 16:18_____

40. Who was Paul's host as he wrote this epistle? 16:23_____

41. How widely is the gospel to be made known?

16:26_____

check-up time No. 6

Review as before, then take the following "true" or "false" test.

1. Paul makes his appeal in Romans 12 on the ground of the mercies of God.   _____

2. One thing we are to prove is that God's will is perfect.   _____

3. Paul says we are to bless those who bless us, and ignore those who persecute us.   _____

4. Kindness to an enemy is apt to make him even more bitter.   _____

5. Every soul is to be subject to the authorities.   _____

6. God sets up good rulers, and Satan wicked ones.   _____

7. The most vital thing in the Christian life is the observation of the Sabbath day.   _____

8. The person who carried Paul's letter to Rome was named Timothy.   _____

9. According to Romans 14, two of the chief matters in dispute in Paul's day were what to eat and what to wear.   _____

10. Paul says Priscilla and Aquila would have given their lives for him, if necessary.   _____

Turn to page 80 and check your answers.

Suggestions for class use

1. The class teacher may wish to tear this page from each workbook as the answer key is on the reverse side.

2. The teacher should study the lesson first, filling in the blanks in the workbook. He should be prepared to give help to the class on some of the harder places in the lesson. He should also take the self-check tests himself, check his answers with the answer key and look up any question answered incorrectly.

3. Class sessions can be supplemented by the teacher's giving a talk or leading a discussion on the subject to be studied. The class could then fill in the workbook together as a group, in teams, or individually. If so desired by the teacher, however, this could be done at home. The self-check tests can be done as homework by the class.

4. The self-check tests can be corrected at the beginning of each class session. A brief discussion of the answers can serve as review for the previous lesson.

5. The teacher should motivate and encourage his students. Some public recognition might well be given to class members who successfully complete this course.

Moody Press, a ministry of the Moody Bible Institute, is designed for education, evangelization and edification. If we may assist you in knowing more about Christ and the Christian life, please write us without obligation to: Moody Press, c/o MLM, Chicago, Illinois 60610.

answer key
to self-check tests

Be sure to look up any questions you answered incorrectly.

Q gives the number of the test *question*.

A gives the correct *answer*.

R *refers* you back to the number of the question in the lesson itself, where the correct answer is to be found.

L refers to the *lesson* from which the question is taken.

Mark with an "x" your wrong answers.

Q	TEST 1 A	R	L	TEST 2 A	R	L	TEST 3 A	R	L
1	T	5	1	T	3	2	F	1	4
2	T	6	1	T	6	2	T	2	4
3	T	7	1	T	7	2	T	6	4
4	T	8	1	F	13	2	T	7	4
5	T	10	1	F	17	2	F	10	4
6	T	13	1	F	23, 24	2	F	5	5
7	F	14	1	T	28	2	T	7	5
8	T	15	1	F	1	3	T	11	5
9	T	22	1	T	18	3	F	12	5
10	F	18	1	T	16	3	F	32	5

Q	TEST 4 A	R	L	TEST 5 A	R	L	TEST 6 A	R	L
1	T	1	6	T	5	9	T	1	11
2	T	7	6	F	7	9	T	6	11
3	T	28	6	F	16	9	F	15	11
4	F	1	7	T	24	9	F	25	11
5	T	23	7	F	28	9	T	26	11
6	T	20	7	F	34	9	F	39	11
7	F	5	8	T	9	10	F	15	12
8	T	15	8	T	22	10	F	33	12
9	F	19	8	F	2	10	F	2, 6	12
10	T	28	8	T	26	10	T	34	12

how well did you do?

0-1 wrong answers—excellent work

2-3 wrong answers—review errors carefully

4 or more wrong answers—restudy the lesson before going on to the next one